Dear Noreen

Thank you so much me to stay & your hospitality. Hopefully will allow you to do an 'armchair' visit to New Zealand.

Love
Gill
April 2004

£2.50
15/8

SEASONS

THE NEW ZEALAND YEAR

NGA WA O TE TAU

SEASONS

THE NEW ZEALAND YEAR

NGA WA O TE TAU

PHOTOGRAPHS BY CRAIG POTTON
TEXT BY DAVID EGGLETON

CRAIG
POTTON
PUBLISHING

Photography © Craig Potton
Text © David Eggleton

Additional photos: p.112 - Photobank Image Library, Roslyn Taylor
p.85 - Chris McLennan/Hedgehog House
pp.66, 113 - Photobank Image Library, Andris Apse

Published by Craig Potton Publishing
98 Vickerman Street, PO Box 555, Nelson, New Zealand
© 2001 Craig Potton Publishing

Printed by PrintLink, Wellington, NZ

ISBN 0-908802-76-5

CONTENTS

INTRODUCTION

The seasons are a calendar charting the cycle of death and rebirth. Since neolithic times, human cultures have observed the seamless progression of life on the planet and woven its rhythms into poetry, myth, and religious and social events. In Aotearoa, traditional Maori culture celebrated the seasons as Takurua (Winter), Mahuru or Koanga (Spring), Raumati (Summer), and Ngahuru (Autumn). They were patterned round the kumara harvest. Though Maori were hunter-gatherers, they also cultivated the land. Te Koanga was the time to dig and plant; the heat of Raumati made the crops grow; Ngahuru was the time of harvest; Takurua was the time when they were sustained by the crops they had harvested.

Seasons may be good, they may be bad, but certainly they are inescapable. We have learnt to live inside the seasons and to read their signs. For some New Zealanders – high country drovers, coastal fishermen and women, lowland farmers – reading the weather signs is essential for survival, they can't afford to be careless. However the meaning and effect of seasons is profound even for urban dwellers. Seasons inform the nation's psychological landscape as well as its physical landscape. Seasons help establish a feeling of belonging. Janet Frame wrote in *A State of Siege* that 'the seasons knew their place in the south', but it is also true that we know our place within the seasons. They are the origin of many of our concepts of beauty, truth, transcendence and spirituality.

New Zealand is a sparsely populated country whose people hug the coasts. We are a nation of fringe-dwellers enjoying the freedom of space, the clarity of the light, the freshness of sea breezes, and even the salt sting of scouring gales. This is a land of freshness, a land wide open to clean air. To walk on an empty Dunedin beach after a big southerly blow has scoured the sand is to feel pure exhilaration. Water purifies, cleanses, washes clean. For New Zealanders the river is within us, as the sea is all around us.

New Zealand is a mountainous country with a

Left: Willow tree, Lake Wakatipu, Queenstown

Above: Late afternoon, Lake Matheson, Westland National Park
Right: Beech forest on the Routeburn Track, Fiordland National Park

mountainous country's weather system. Much of the landscape is hilly, withdrawn and silent, a place of muscular, sinewy ridges. Our mountains, geologically young, are constantly replenished by upheavals. They are dynamic and volatile like the everchanging weather patterns. Within an hour a caressing breeze can change into a lashing gale.

This is a place where the earth's crust buckles and tilts dramatically as two globe-girdling tectonic plates scrunch up against one another. A fracture zone of faultlines extends along much of the narrow length of the country, pushing up earthworks of gigantic grandeur. The mountains are of operatic proportions, Wagnerian stage sets for vast geological dramas. In Fiordland, the mountains are like forested walls, diving almost vertically into the sea. Writhing river valleys plunge from jagged ridges, and along them great exclamations of water career recklessly downhill towards shingle beaches pounded by ocean rollers.

New Zealand is a landscape of contrasts, of dissonances, aural as well as visual. Stand on the tongue of the Franz Josef glacier in the summer thaw and hear the ice groan and rumble and squeal with pressure as it contracts; then wander down the main street of almost any small town on a Sunday morning and listen to the silence, to the emptiness.

New Zealand is a world in miniature. Driving across the South Island in a single day, you can take in an astonishing number of climatic and physical variations. Cool west Otago beach, damp east Otago montane bog, the dry craggy tor of the Central Otago schist plateau, the ice-ploughed tussock-covered hills round the glacial lakes of Wakatipu, Wanaka and Hawea, the beech-forested mountains of the Alps, the glowering gorges leading to the sunny river flats of the Haast coastal plain, with its kahikatea rainforest and the moody Tasman Sea beyond.

New Zealand is a land of plenty, offering earth's bounty: it's not only a primary producer, a pastoral powerhouse of meat, wool and milk, but also an ecological wonderland. More than 80 percent of New Zealand's flowering plants are found nowhere else in the world.

We are also part of a small planet, subject to the millennial rhythms of climate change, from ice age to hothouse age and back again. Here, at the beginning of the twenty-first century we seem to be in a hothouse phase. There are events and processes in nature independent of the seasonal calendar, which nevertheless interrupt and alter cycles of growth. These events

Right: Winter on the road to Lake Ohau, Mackenzie Country

– earthquakes, tidal waves, volcanic activity – have always affected human society. Now they have been joined by the phenomenon of global warming making weather patterns more erratic.

Over the past century, the world's average surface temperature has been steadily going up. Over the next few decades the temperature could rise by up to five degrees or more. In New Zealand this has already led to more storms approaching out of the west, with less rain falling on the sheltered east coast, while more rain falls on the exposed west coast. Although Gisborne, Hawke's Bay and Marlborough are becoming drier and hotter, the West Coast of the South Island, Taranaki and Auckland are becoming wetter and hotter. In some regions, frequent bouts of heavy rain cause flash floods. Coastal wetlands are under threat from rising sea levels. The increasing warmth will lead to a change in the balance of species in forests as some cope better with the heat than others. In Canterbury, the end of the twentieth century was marked by the hottest July temperatures ever recorded, though there were local variations. Scientists tell us that since the mid-nineteenth century up to a third of the permanent snow and ice on the Southern Alps has been lost.

Meanwhile the deeper rhythms of the seasons persist – spring floods, sunny summers, golden autumns, white winters. We live in an exuberant country which bulks into the clouds, cutting the clear sky with clean lines. It's lit by strong sunshine, watched over by brooding volcanoes. It's still a land of 'nestling ports and precarious settlements' as Maurice Shadbolt wrote years ago, a primeval mountain range archipelago charging up out of the sea, tamed here and there by pastoral farms, orchards, market gardens, even a scatter of cities, but still wild at the centre of its being.

Right: Autumn evening, Tahunanui Beach, Nelson

Above: High summer, Richardson Mountains, West Otago
Right: Lake Mapourika, Westland National Park

SUMMER

RAUMATI

Summer is our fire season, but it builds slowly and sometimes erratically: the pattern of endless warm days tempered by rain storms is subject to change without notice. There may be no rain for weeks and weeks, and meanwhile everything catches the sun. Iridescent feathers of birds brush the blue sky. Ocean waves are strokes of silver; mouths of rivers turn to molten gold. Mountain ice melts under sun's heat. Shining creeks lace through cloaks of green. Grasslands dry out and begin to fade to brown.

The official beginning of summer in New Zealand is December 1. The brilliant lights of the Scorpius constellation to the west have faded in the night sky. In the east Orion is just rising and the Southern Cross is barely scraping the horizon. As the sun comes up, the rays of the new dawn crown the head of Hikurangi, the highest mountain in the Raukumara Range on the East Cape of the North Island, before flooding the entire land.

For farmers, the working day starts early and finishes late, and summer sees them shift into top gear. The spring muster has brought the sheep in. Millions

Left: Southeastern shore of Lake Taupo

of them have been driven down from tilted blocks of hill country and onto paddocks fenced by four or five galvanised wire strands strung on fence battens, sometimes leaning at all angles, running out from old, cracked, lichen-covered strainer posts. In these paddocks the sheep mob up, baaing and bleating, or calmly chewing cud and nibbling grass.

The other creature with a lead role to play is the sheep dog – the heading dog, the backing dog, the huntaway. A whistle or a word are enough to convey a precise order and to control the intricate manoeuvrings that bring a whole mob of sheep through a series of gates and into the exact pens required.

The sheep and their lambs have to be led through shower-dip or sheep-race and given a dose of drench to protect them against fly-strike, lice and worms. Lambs are weighed, ear-marked, and, if male, castrated. They are also weaned, have their tails docked and are drafted for fattening up, especially in evergreen regions like Southland and the Waikato.

Lambs destined for the freezing works, or for on-selling to other farms, are off the farm by about four months of age. At lamb fairs, held in December and January, the fattening farmers, having sold their prime

lambs, purchase drafts of unfattened sheep from hill country farms. Leaning on wooden rails at stock saleyards, the fit, rangy farmers jut their jaws and calculate prices with set expressions, not giving too much away.

Summer is the time of one of the great climaxes of the farming calendar – sheep shearing. In early December the shearing gangs arrive. Toiling in woolsheds, shearers are soon coated in sweat and smeared with lanolin oils from the fleeces. Shed hands cope with fleece after fleece, sorting them and cramming them into bales. Heavy rainfall is especially unwelcome at this time, as fleeces become muddied

Above: Summer shearing
Left: Late summer, North Canterbury

and matted.

Out in the paddocks, after a dry spell, the crusting of ripe seedheads offers evidence the grass is ready to be made into hay. Soon cylinders or bales of golden wispy straw dot the landscape in neat geometrical patterns, before being dragged into tin sheds or piled under polythene.

Dairy farmers wake early most days of the year, getting milking underway in the pre-dawn darkness. They employ a complex schedule of mating, calving and calf-rearing to ensure a steady supply of milk.

Cows are grazed by rotation in a series of paddocks to ease pressure on pasture growth. In places where grass grows lush and green, such as Taranaki or the Waikato, farmers also need to keep a keen eye on greedy cows: too much fermented grass causes them to blow up with gas, a potentially fatal condition.

While many paddocks are shorn for hay in January, on the patchwork quilt of the Canterbury Plains – the nation's granary belt – bulk-harvester combines are cutting and threshing the billowing wheat crop for flour-milling. In roadside fields, honeybees are fossicking amongst drifts of yellow buttercups or white clover flowers. The scent of clover is mingled with the sweet-and-sour reek of fresh silage, fermenting in the hot weather in tarpaulin-covered pits. Summer on New Zealand's long narrow islands is intense but unsettled. As wind ruffles shelter-belts, the heads of farm animals may be observed cocked in anticipation of a cool change.

Summer intensifies and coastal regions become humid. The day's rhythms are determined by the rise and fall of tides and by morning and evening breezes that start up fitfully then die away. The warm ocean air which is not dispelled turns muggy, and in some eastern places – Tauranga, Whakatane – it's like living

Above: Rangipo Desert, Tongariro National Park
Right: Lake Matheson, Westland National Park

seals are sleeping in the sun, and the mountains, so far, yet so near, seem to float above the sea mist. On these fine days the waves are gleaming blue and green with sculpted crests as white as enamel paint. Coming out of the complex of inlets which is the Marlborough Sounds and scooting away from the Inter-Islander ferry, a yacht's white sail is a joyous message thrust into the bottleneck of Cook Strait where flecked waves pound beneath the wind.

Up north, weeks of sultry weather may set in before easterlies finally bring rain to the sheltered coves of Northland.

In Auckland a few people go for a swim in the sea on Labour Day in October, but it is not until summer that the North Shore's beaches, each pinned to the green coastline like a ragged golden ribbon, boast throngs of sunseekers. In mid-December, city workers anticipate the approach of Christmas and New Year – the traditional break – with office parties. As school ends, young children get taken by parents or grandparents to paddle in the translucent crystal waters of the gentle inner city beaches, while older teenagers often drive to the wild west coast beaches of Piha, Muriwai and Karekare. In these places westerly storms are apt to rage, blowing up suddenly out of a clear sky.

in a steambath where everything damp seems in danger of developing algal bloom. Hawke's Bay on the other hand, close, windless and sweltering in dry heat, can resemble a sweatbox. But an easterly or southerly breeze starts up, gathers a sweet cooling force, and the tension lifts, the mood lightens.

In cooler regions like the South Island coasts where there are warm currents just offshore, a salt-laden haze hangs above the beaches. On the rocks,

Above: Pasifika Festival, Auckland
Right: Mission Bay, Auckland

22

Above: Nor'west cloud over Lake Pukaki and Aoraki/Mt Cook
Right: Mist covering Nor'west Lake, Fiordland National Park

Top: Beach cricket
Above: Surfing competition, Gisborne
Right: Boys and boats, Golden Bay

On a sparkling summer's day, Auckland's optical pleasures come into their own: the choice perspectives; the interpenetration of sea, land, and sky in dazzling combinations; the skewed perspectives of the skinny isthmus; the trowelled-on true light of the Pacific, bright and clear and breeze-driven. The weather does change suddenly: sunlight fluxing from minute to minute as masses of cloud roll in. There's a sudden temperature drop. Thunder begins rumbling. Suddenly you're hit by raindrops. Sun-heated gravel hisses with steam. The whole landscape seems to be breathing and alive. Waterspouts are rising out on the horizon, clouds are dropping towards the sea. The waterspouts start to move shorewards, then, as suddenly as they rose, they break apart, splintering into spun flecks and vanishing.

It's a storm symphony: kettledrum thunder, raindrops like plucked violin strings, a brass band impetuousness as rain builds, sudden gusts like the quick clamour of wood instruments. Windows swim with water; you expect to see fish flapping past as the downpour becomes relentless, cannonading off corrugated iron roofs in the suburbs, tumbling into concrete canyons in the city, the rain one swirling mass of animation. Just as suddenly, it's all over. The

sky is an intense blue as the last clouds sweep imperiously off into the distance, like great white pointer sharks. After the rain, the volcanic earth of Auckland is spongy, tropical. The plant life is quivering, brimming, as the humidity begins to climb again. Evenings bring lurid sunsets with a natural dimmer switch attached.

New Zealand is a water-loving country, a land that produces champion sailors, rowers and windsurfers. The Auckland Anniversary Weekend Yachting Regatta in January has become the largest amateur yachting regatta in the world.

Summer is also the time for surf-casters. The bounty of Tangaroa, god of the sea, increases as fish come close inshore to spawn. Up and down the coasts, people fish for kai moana – mackerel, snapper, barracuda – to put on the table. Dolphins are fishing too, splashing through the sea, herding shoals together and then feeding on them. In the deep south, oyster boats, with drag nets of chain mesh and rope cordage, dredge for oysters in late summer/early autumn.

In summer the land and the people are self-possessed, replete and ripened. As the Christmas break approaches and the snow and tinsel of Christmas cards begin to crowd the mantelpiece, end-of-year torpor

Top: Polynesian dancers at Pasifika Festival, Auckland
Above: Pohutukawa tree in full flower, Little Barrier Island, Hauraki Gulf
Left: Summer shower over Skytower and central Auckland

causes collar-and-tie formality to be relaxed. For townies it's the start of the slack season. After a year of hard yacker it's time for a laze at the beach or beside a lake. The summer solstice (falling between 20 and 23 December) sees holidays beginning. Holiday-makers red-legged, peach-fuzzed and sun-ripened reach for sunblock and sunhat, but often only after a fair bit of skin has peeled off.

Around the country the rasp of cicadas has begun to tickle the ear of summer. In sedate suburbs the emerald effulgence of bowling lawns is the setting where teams of bowlers, young and old, kitted out in crisp, white uniforms launch into competitions. Down unsealed roads in the centre of the North Island, white pumice dust is rising in clouds behind cars as bushed office workers migrate to holiday hideaways. Overnight, deserted motor-camps become busy tent towns. Soon holiday-makers are putting in long hours in togs, blowing up lilos, dripping ice creams on themselves, or cooking mussels and pipis on corrugated iron over a beach fire and wondering if they can wear their togs and worn-down jandals away from the beach.

On the beaches of Paihia, Mount Maunganui and Tahunanui, regional lifeguard patrols, most of them volunteers, are visible between the flags or on jetskis on the water. Enthusiastic volleyball and cricket players claim beach turf for themselves. Surfers are parked up along beachfronts in their clapped-out station wagons or rebuilt Big Sixes – Holdens, Falcons, Valiants – scoping out the waves.

Some visitors to the beach are more languid, afflicted with the devotional contemplation of their own suntans, or are content to sit under flapping tent awnings nursing a beer and contemplating the old year clicking over into the new, while offspring are intently trying to catch cockabullies in rock pools.

In cities, as hot January gives way to hotter

Above: Sailing on the Waitemata Harbour
Right: Summer cricket match

February, the air is like consommé, a tepid soup of fumes. Inland towns bask like lizards. Motorists face the hazard of "summer ice" – spilt diesel rising through the bitumen to the surface of the road and making it greasy. On summer evenings trees, buildings and moving objects seem to float in the twilight with a special clarity. At night, the warm air is like liquid velvet. Against the background of the night, the ruby, gold and blue of neon signage gleam with a soft lustre. Away from the city lights, on the Coromandel peninsula for instance, where tiny indigenous frogs chirp from magnificent remnants of native bush, Magellanic clouds twinkle in the heavens like specks of tinsel, and the tails of shooting stars can be seen.

Mid to late summer is the time when food festival succeeds food festival in a mood of upbeat, almost frantic celebration, as taste buds battle with an almost overwhelming cornucopia of tastes and flavours. Thus New Zealand is confirmed as one of the world's centres of boutique food enthusiasm. "She (or he) does a good pavlova" is still a benchmark of praise, but what baroque garnishings and fixings now surround the national dish!

The flush of the season is expressed in fantastic

Top: Cooling off, Abel Tasman National Park
Above: Escaping the summer heat, Whanganui River
Left: Sand dunes, Wharariki, west coast of Golden Bay

By mid-summer, viticulturalists are trimming vine canopies and plucking away leaves from ripening grape clusters. In Marlborough, while hills dry out under the perennial drought conditions, the mix of cool nights and warm days on irrigated plains is perfect for rieslings, chardonnays and sauvignon blancs. The grape-growing climate of Hawke's Bay is said to be nearly identical to that of the Bordeaux region in France, and North Otago's is said to mimic Burgundy's.

Nelson produces wine but is best known for apples, harvested from mid-February to late April when breezes are gentle and the heat beats down. The delicate, haunting blossom of spring resolves into firm fruit with russet, pink, pale green, or dark red skins. Apples are gathered in aprons, baskets and cases by a tribe of seasonal workers.

In the cool forests, light filters through into the depths as if through stained glass windows. Scarlet, orange and dark purple berries are fruiting high in the native trees – matai, totara, tawa, kahikatea, miro and karaka trees. Once such berries provided a feast for Maori. The exuberance of the pre-European forest world was recorded by the explorer Thomas Brunner who wrote: 'In December ... the rivers, large or small

harvests: feijoas, macadamias, pawpaws and persimmons in the far north; wasabi, walnuts, quinces, medlars, chestnuts and artichokes on Banks Peninsula; cherries, apricots, nectarines and peaches in Central Otago. At harvest time, the kitchens of the entire country seem to be dominated by fruit bowls and vege bins. There's a spud festival in the south and a kumara festival in the north. Meanwhile, the reserve bins of our wineries groan under the weight of international gold and silver medals.

Above: The Gathering, an annual summer music festival, near Nelson
Right: Surfers near Gisborne

Above: Sunset over the South Island, Kapiti Coast
Right: Vineyard heavy with summer growth, Marlborough

abound in eels, hawera, upukuroro, hapuru, patiki, and parauki. The fruit of the kiekie is then ripe, called by the natives tawara, and is very luscious, more like a conserve than a fruit. The honey of the flax blossom is also in season, and, when mixed with fern fruit, also makes a species of confectionery.'

Trampers escaping into national parks from the summer glare experience the gamut of greens of the myriad bush ferns. High up, the rata vine displays its white, orange or crimson flowers. Garlands of native mistletoe encircle beech trees with red flowers. Dragonflies hover like miniature helicopters above greenish-grey marsh pools, surrounded by rows of reddish-brown reeds.

The dark red flowers of the pohutukawa tree and the brighter red flowers of the southern rata tree are closely related and have been our traditional festive blooms ever since the Reverend Samuel Marsden conducted New Zealand's first Christmas Day service on a beach in the Bay of Islands in 1814 within sight of blossoming pohutukawa trees. When in flower, pohutukawa are musical: they are filled with the murmur of bees, and the trees produce a honey which is very white. Nowadays, the red spray of the pohutukawa is less common up north. Farming has

Top: Flower of the pohutukawa, often called the New Zealand Christmas tree
Above: Marlborough rock daisy
Right: Mixed podocarp forest, Whirinaki, Central North Island

eliminated more than 90 percent of northern coastal pohutukawa stands, while voracious possums have made bare, bleached skeletons of many of the remaining pohutukawa.

Another introduced species which pesters forests, in cahoots with possums, goats and assorted mustelids, is the wasp. Besides making a nuisance of themselves round fruit trees, wasps also plague beech forests, feeding on honeydew, the sugary secretion produced by scale insects which live on the bark of beech trees. The honeydew is also much sought after by native insects, who are in turn fed on by native birds. The buzzing of millions of wasps in the beech forests, though, may have reached its crescendo as the population explosion appears to be over.

Any population explosion is definitely over for the native bats of South Canterbury. Sightings of the formerly widespread, winged, furry mammals, who once swarmed in the skies over the limestone caves of forested regions, are now very rare. Enormous numbers of moths and butterflies, however, continue to flutter through the air. On warm nights moths crowd round porch lights which are left on or dash themselves blindly against car headlights.

By late January/early February, the drought-prone

parts of New Zealand are being anxiously scrutinised. Often resembling unglazed, biscuit-fired earthenware in colour and texture, these sunburnt regions can literally go up in flames at the drop of a match. The nor'wester, a wind hot as a baking oven, can cause even controlled burn-offs to run amok. Over the spicy earth of the tussocklands comes a red-gold girdle of fire to leave behind sour, blackened ash pits. Fires regularly and mysteriously start up close to towns, on

Above: Summer cloud build up, Lake Tekapo, Mackenzie Country
Left: Gannet colony, Muriwai, Auckland's west coast

flanks of hills with pockets of gorse in flower, leading to crackling infernos which appear on the television news. Helicopters allow close-up footage of fire dragons leaping up gullies or down towards houses to be filmed as gorse bushes explode into balls of flame.

In the far north in late summer another brute phenomenon can arise: the tropical cyclone. These humdingers are generated in the tropical latitudes and sometimes move down towards New Zealand travelling above exceptionally warm sea currents. They often transform themselves along the way, blowing out or fading into heavy rainstorms. Sometimes, however, they arrive as a full-blown lethal sideswipe of a storm. The most famous examples have been Cyclone Bola, which wreaked exceptional devastation around the North Island's East Cape in March, 1988, and Cyclone Giselle, which contributed to the sinking of the inter-island ferry Wahine in Wellington Harbour, with the loss of 51 people in April, 1968.

So summer, the seasonal home of the pleasure principle, is fickle. An ocean played on by sunlight – now a delicate indigo, now freckled with fire – may stir in its black depths and perhaps crash with a late surge of fury onto the shore.

Left: Sea kayaking, Abel Tasman National Park

AUTUMN

NGAHURU

Autumn: a cat's-paw ruffle on a lake breaking up a reflected mosaic of deciduous trees; tendrils of lightning illuminating a dark storm on the volcanic plateau; a clutch of albatross feathers drenched in mist.

Autumn officially begins on the first day of March, but the long, hot days only start to ebb away gradually. For a few weeks there's an indian summer, not quite true autumn yet, but cooler than before. The dew on the grass deepens, especially in humid regions. The clear days and still nights become somehow more wistful. Then you begin to sense something of the flat weight of the earth, its loss, its slippage. Yet autumn is also busy with a new urgency as last fruits and crops are harvested before the first cold snap.

Creatures of all kinds begin journeying to their winter homes. There's a quivering and a rustling in the trees, then the wind showers us with abrupt gifts: a first yellow leaf or a last tiny blossom. Pinecones clunk to the ground and roll into the long grass ready to be gathered up for winter fireplaces. The evening sun, tracking across the sea, sinks out of sight, leaving a smoky-orange moon on the rise.

Left: Autumn morning, near Nelson

In the night sky, Venus – autumn's faithful planet of the twilight – shines brightly. The Southern Cross constellation twinkles high in the heavens. For traditional Maori, who were careful astronomers, this was the time of the kumara harvest. The atua or star Whanui (also known as Vega) which first appears in the night sky in February, was the kumara god. Once, there was no kumara on earth: it belonged in the sky and was always guarded by Whanui. Then, Rongo-matane male god of the moon (his symbol is the crescent) stole up to Whanui's kumara house and took some kumara to share out amongst mortals. From that time forth, when the kumara crop was lifted, karakia were chanted at dawn by a tohunga and the first tubers were cooked in a sacred fire and offered to the male and female gods of the harvest moon.

In the animistic universe of traditional Maori, the world was holistic: it moved according to the rhythm of nature. Omens, such as a lightning flash over a tapu mountain, were read as warnings. Failure to maintain harmony with the forces of the natural world would lead to loss of mana, and, ultimately, catastrophe.

Autumn is still a time for root crops. There are turnips, swedes, parsnips, carrots and potatoes, as well as kumara. Some of these vegetables will be given to

Above: Late autumn snowfall, Mt Taranaki, Egmont National Park
Left: Foothills of the Southern Alps, near Okarito

farm animals as winter feed, some will be sold through supermarkets and end up in stews, roasts and casseroles, and some will be trucked to ports for export to Asia and elsewhere. In market-garden sheds, autumnal crops of peas, radishes, cauliflowers, onions, broccoli and beans are sorted and bagged. On lowland farms, tractors pull harrows back and forth cultivating the soil for spring crops – wheat, barley, potatoes, carrots, silverbeet and lettuce. These slowly moving tractors are often attended by small flocks of birds eager for the earthworms that the ploughing turns up. The pasturelands become a patchwork of sown surfaces.

In the vineyards of Martinborough, Marlborough and elsewhere, grape pickers are hard at work amongst the burdened vines. The speckled, white, purple and dark red spheres that form the vintage are hand- or machine-harvested at different times in different places. The Gisborne harvest takes place in early March while the cycle finishes in Central Otago in May. By then, all the wine-makers will have shifted inside to their wineries to begin pressing and fermenting the grape juice into vinous nectar.

The glut of fresh fruit at harvest time keeps canneries busy and provides the raw materials for the

Above: Grape pickers, Marlborough
Right: Sauvignon blanc crop, Marlborough

home bottling and preserving and the making of jams and chutney that is still practised. Increasingly, jars of home-style preserves are being sold commercially on both local and overseas markets.

In forests, native plants are producing the last of their colourful berries, fruits and seeds. You can see orange karaka berries, red nikau palm berries and black seeds emerging from flax pods. Fungi flourish on the damp forest floors. Crackled-brown puffballs, porcelain-blue toadstools, the lurid-lilac *Hygrophorus* fungus and the *Mycena* fungus with its glistening, crème brûlée tints are on display. The cascades of creamy-white blooms produced by the late-flowering lacebark (houhere) are a floral highlight of the autumnal rainforest. To the north, the powhiwhi covers sheltered north-facing hillsides with tangles of brilliant flowers. On the mudflat estuaries of the sub-tropical north, and as far south as Ohiwa on the east coast and Raglan on the west, lichen-draped mangroves (manawa) begin producing their tiny pink flowers.

One of the subtle aromas of the evergreen New Zealand bush in autumn is the fragrance of wild orchids. These highly-developed plants have elaborately arranged flowers in order to attract fickle pollinating insects such as the native bee. Some

orchids, competing for attention, have evolved a powerful scent. The Easter orchid (raupeka), flowering in April, has an overwhelming, almost cloying, perfume that clings to you even before you see the flowers.

The autumn equinox occurs between 20 and 23 March and frequently signals the arrival of strong winds. The boom and rattle of wind gusts around an old weatherboard house is one of the haunting sounds of autumn. Winds can be especially strong in the

Above: Autumn light
Left: Mountain ribbonwood, one of New Zealand's few deciduous native trees

lower half of the North Island, in the Wairarapa Valley and in the streets of Wellington, where the umbrellas of public servants may sometimes be observed blowing inside out. Down on Lambton Quay or on The Terrace, everything looks windblown or sandblasted, and the air is full of flying grit, discarded food packaging and tumbling sheets of newspaper. Flapping branches of trees are trying to shake off their leaves, and scurrying commuters look for shelter or hunch down into their overcoats.

The russet leaves on exotic trees – poplars, willows, oaks, birches and larches – begin to gradually fall and pile up in deep drifts in parks and gardens. Gardeners begin raking them together for compost or for bonfires. Leaves are raked out of gutters and cleared from roof drainpipes. Everywhere south of Hamilton the keynote green colour leaches from the leafy vegetation of the pastoral landscape and is replaced by a rhapsody of umber, sienna, rose, yellow, red and pink. These leaf pigments, whose job it is to protect the green chlorophyll from excessive radiation during summer, now come into their own as the arboreal mechanisms of photosynthesis go into hibernation. They blaze their colours, float like confetti to the ground, and begin to decay, fading to muted tones then into invisibility, in accordance with the seasonal cycle. The last of the Russell lupins are like clusters of coloured popcorn along roadside verges, but within a matter of days these fluttering flowers, too, will all be gone.

Now, in the stillness of early morning, fog lies along cool river valleys and mist clings to hilltops, etching the outline of each ridge. Seen from the air, the North Island hill country is a smudge of blue pastel colours – teal, aquamarine and the saturated dark primary blue known as cyan.

In late autumn the great annual migration of eels takes place from inland lakes and rivers to the sea.

Above: Silvery light from an autumn snowstorm, Lake Te Anau
Left: Golden poplars, Kawerau River, Queenstown

They congregate in the deep pools of the remote bush before slithering their way downstream under cover of darkness. Offshore, the schools of young snapper spawned in summer are now full-grown and will linger inshore for only a few weeks more before moving to warmer waters for winter. Terakihi, however, are still schooling and spawning close to shore during autumn. White-fronted terns, wheeling and diving in flocks, tell the trolling fisher where to drop the line. During late April and May, moki migrate from off Kaikoura up to the coast between Mahia Peninsula and East Cape to spawn. Further up the coast, at the mouth of the big Motu river, Maori gather to net the run of kahawai that occurs there once a year. In the deep-sea trench off Kaikoura crayfish begin to spawn.

Autumn is an active time for inland anglers. In April, the quiet flow of many high country streams is alive with spawning salmon and brown trout. Rainbow trout spawn a few weeks later. All these freshwater fish prefer to spawn in the higher, cooler reaches of the streams that straggle out of the mountains. As the fish travel upstream, anglers are waiting, casting for glimmerings, while the speckled trout, their shadows moving beneath them, ripple through river displays of light and shade – mid-stream crystal, purl-

ing shallows, churning waterfalls. In South Canterbury, anglers fish for quinnat salmon, alert to their sudden flash of silver in the milky-green of the Waitaki River.

The long-tailed and shining cuckoos (koekoea and pipiwharauroa) begin to set off for tropic latitudes almost before autumn arrives. Most other birds, however, plan their departure for a little later. Estuaries are crowded. Large flocks skein the coastal skies executing aerial manoeuvres. The inner Firth of Thames teems with activity as a host of international avian

Above: Early morning cloud, Malte Brun Range, Aoraki/Mount Cook National Park.
Left: Nor'west cloud over The Remarkables Range and foothills, Queenstown

visitors bulk up for the long haul. The birds feed on the tiny crustaceans of the fertile mudflats that stretch in a long curve of coast from Kaiaua to the mouths of the Piako and Waihou Rivers.

Twice each day, the migrant waders of the Thames estuary are forced off the mudflats by the tide and find refuge on the beaches and shellbanks of the foreshore. Pied stilts leap from the advancing waves with a flurry. They glide up into the air, then back down to land going for short runs along the beach. Pied oystercatchers tend to amble, making a sharp pip-pip call. Banded dotterels run silently on dainty legs in a low-slung, quick-stepping fashion. Red-billed gulls wander nonchalantly amongst them. When they aren't stalking the tidal flats for food, assorted curlews, godwits, sandpipers and knots may be seen just quietly spending time preening or dozing with their heads tucked under one wing. If the wind is blowing, they tend to stand on one leg to conserve body heat.

Most of these birds travel to Siberia and the Arctic Circle in order to breed during the northern summer. As the time to leave approaches, male birds start to develop breeding plumage. The greyish-brown and white dotterels grow red chest feathers; the fawn-coloured godwits and the knots turn russet, while the brown turnstones take on a speckled tortoise-shell colouring. By late March, flocks are beginning to amass on the estuaries of the northern half of the North Island, staining the sky in their thousands. Many bar-tailed godwits (New Zealand's most common migrant wader) gather on the Kaipara Harbour or assemble at Spirits Bay on Cape Reinga. Godwits launch endless training flights. Then all at once they've gone, off to the top of the world via China, Korea and Japan. They will spend about a month en route.

In autumn birds everywhere are on the move. Though hard to spot even close up, iridescent native wood-pigeons (kereru) are flying noisily amongst the remnants of indigenous lowland forest in search of the remaining fruits of the forest. Above farm pastures, the evening skies are full of birds flying low to catch the insects rising from the pasturelands. Duck populations shift from upland lakes to coastal lagoons for winter. Kingfishers come down from the hills to warmer zones. White-faced herons, Australian welcome swallows, and many other birds take up winter coastal residencies. Meanwhile, white-fronted terns are amongst those leaving for the eastern seaboard of Australia. South Island pied oystercatchers, which breed in the South Island high country in spring, fly to

Right: A still autumn evening on Nelson Haven

albatross clacks with affirmation before the bird soars from the bleak promontory on an updraught, its great wing-span shadowing first the ground, then the sea below, as it glides away. Perhaps it will not touchdown on land again for months.

Elsewhere on the peninsula, yellow-eyed penguins (hoiho) plod doggedly across the sand as night falls, scrambling up the dunes to their roosts amongst clumps of flax. There, the hoiho's downy offspring wait to learn the arts of survival before themselves launching into the sea in late autumn.

Swarms of sooty shearwaters (muttonbirds or titi) are on the wing, migrating to other Pacific islands. Their great multitudes resemble a delicate embroidery of vast parabolas rising and falling to become a shading of dots in the distance. Maori muttonbirders claim a tiny percentage of these birds during the muttonbirding season which commences in April and ceases in mid-May, when most of the birds have departed. By that time, thousands of chicks will have been taken from their burrows. Their necks are wrung, or bitten through, and the birds are then plucked, salted and packed in seaweed bags. Others, cooked in their own fat, are feasted on immediately. Muttonbirding has gone on for hundreds of years and is as

northern coastal harbours in autumn to replace the departing godwits. Not all godwits leave however. Younger ones who are not ready for breeding may winter over in New Zealand.

Traditional Maori looked on their going as a departure of spirits to the underworld. Birds were the souls of the dead or messengers of the gods: either way they were travellers to metaphysical realms.

In seabird nesting areas, young gulls are earning their wings and beginning to soar high. Fledglings attract the attention of predatory harrier hawks which must be driven off by the adult gulls. On Otago Peninsula, the big, hooked bill of the mature wandering much an act of cultural continuity as the consumption of a sought-after delicacy.

May heralds open season on ducks. For a limited time, on estuaries, rivers, lagoons and lakes, the mallard, native grey duck, paradise shelduck (putangitangi), black swan and the Canada goose may be decoyed, stalked, hunted and shot. Perhaps over the generations the birds have developed an awareness of this, as bird sanctuaries around the country fill up with these game birds at this time of year.

Spring lambs are weaned in autumn and are now called hoggets. They are often sold off at hogget fairs. Calves have also been weaned and may be sold at weaner fairs, bought by lowland farmers for rapid fattening and an early dispatch to the abattoirs. Beef cattle are sold in autumn as well. Whole herds often change owners at large-scale cattle fairs. Ewes are mated in autumn to ensure that lambing begins just as the spring grass is growing through.

To the north Auckland is usually, though not always, enjoying what North Shore poet A.R.D. Fairburn called 'soft April Weather'. In the South Island the wheat farmers are anxiously awaiting late-autumn rains. As Eileen Duggan wrote in her poem *The Farming Nation*:

Above: Yellow-eyed penguin (boiho) coming ashore, South Otago coast
Left: Sooty shearwater (muttonbird)
Far left: Godwits gather, preparing for their annual migration to Siberia

He and weather have a meaning for each other
In a city, rain lies barren in a street,
But a farmer's rain is married to his paddocks
And a farmer's sun is mid-wife to his wheat.

Across farmlands, the smoke from scrub burn-offs
tinges the light of the sun and creeks are sluggish. In
the inland South Island the dog days of the howling
nor'wester can turn everyone irritable. The classic

Canterbury nor'wester is a phenomenon of summer
and autumn, but it can occur at any time. After a spell
of calm, fine weather, the air pressure will suddenly
drop and an arch of cumulus clouds forms over the
mountain ranges to the north-west. This spectacular
white cloud arch is separated from the mass of low
nimbus clouds hanging over the mountains by a
segment of cloudless, deep-blue sky which has a
peculiar soft haze to it. Soon, the wind begins to blow

Above: Fishing for trout, Waitahanui, Lake Taupo
Right: Mt Tasman and Aoraki/Mt Cook viewed from the west, Westland National Park

more strongly out of the north-west.

Where there has been little or no rain for several weeks, river beds begin to dry up and the silt becomes the raw material for a stifling dust storm. Dust whirls into every nook and cranny as the howling nor'wester sweeps across the plains, dragging with it the latent heat stored in the ground over summer. On these dry plains, stressed by heat and wind, irrigation becomes important. Water is pumped up from aquifers deep in the shingle layers of the soil. Big mobile

irrigators, revolving like huge rotary clotheslines, spray up to 1200 litres of water a minute onto the parched earth.

Eventually, the wind dies down or changes direction, as cooler air starts to flow up from southern regions in response to the hot blasts. Often these southerlies bring rain. If the responding wind is a sou'westerly, however, it may just be cool and dry. Sometimes when a nor'wester dies down the evening that follows is hot and still. The dry air clarifies objects on the horizon such as farmhouses, silos and shelterbelts. The far-off mountains loom large and lordly, surrounded by white ruffs of cloud. There may be the smell of cabbage tree blossom withering and falling, sun-baked tussock or the acrid tang of burnt gorse.

The phenomenon of the nor'wester has helped establish some record-breaking altitudes for glider flights. Gliding clubs have annual meets in the Mackenzie Country in autumn, when they use the updraughts of the nor'west wind to carry their lightweight planes to empyrean heights.

Autumn is also the time of the South Island fall muster, when sheep are brought down from the high ranges having been trailed after the receding snowline

Above: Arable farming, south of Wanganui
Right: Rainbow near Lindis Pass, Mackenzie Country

all summer. Nowadays, four-wheel-drives, trail bikes and even helicopters are used to round up the sheep, reducing a process that used to take weeks to a matter of days. A clean muster of these high country merino flocks is essential because any sheep left behind are unlikely to survive the winter.

In autumn, apart from the intermittent rattle of rubble down shingle screes, the high alpine country is a withdrawn and silent land. This landscape is suffused with shades of purple, grey and bronze, out of which a tangle of turquoise threads descend to the coast. Below the perpetual snows of the Southern Alps, the white-petalled flowers of mountain lilies and butter-cups linger on. Amongst the alpine riverbeds, "vegeta-ble sheep" manage to flourish, protected from the extreme climate by their tiny, close-packed leaves, which are in turn insulated with a network of fine threads resembling silvery felt. These plants turn brown in late autumn, as if going into hibernation for winter.

Dark specks of keas spiral against the sky, above steep slopes framed by teetering rock ridges. In a sheltered cushion bog, the sticky liquids of an alpine sundew plant snare a blue damsel fly. The mirrored sheen of an upland tarn reflects a sunset which is giving the Alps a pink tinge. Down below, the warm flanks of the Central Otago ranges glow tan and blond, orange and gold. The scent of the last of the wild thyme drifts across hillsides. With slow, patient wingbeats, a hungry harrier hawk criss-crosses a hillside. Farmhouse lights come on at the end of gravel roads. The ripples of the Clutha River, gurgling along, are lost in the gathering gloom. On the coastal fringe of the Caitlins Forest Park, waters drain from peat bogs, tumble down cliff faces and move on into the lengthening shadows of the night.

Left: Morning in May, Auckland Harbour Bridge and the Waitemata Harbour
Overleaf: Autumn muster, Dunstan Downs Station, Central Otago

WINTER

TAKURUA

High drama. The sky grizzles and weeps. Rain-shrouded hills brood. Scudding mists cover and uncover water, rock and forest. Trees in national parks hunker down against the elements. Creatures of all kinds take to their bolt-holes. Icy gales hector farmers. The sacrificial altars of abattoirs and freezing works echo and are stark.

Winter begins officially on the first day of June, and the month itself usually brings fogs and rain ahead of the heavy storms of July. As chill winds blow up from the southern ocean, temperatures gradually drop over the land. July is often ushered in by a snowstorm: tiny ice particles in the stratosphere coalescing and drifting earthward. Mist, cloud, snowflakes – winter winches snowy peaks into view out of a perfect flurry of white. Alpine steeps become great absolutes of snow and ice. Mountains emerge as high and mighty presences that no New Zealander can ignore.

When the skies clear again, the landscape is in the grip of winter. Winter's heart seems as delicate as the chandeliers of sticky threads strung by glow-worms in a cave. Winter hangs transparent icicles from the bare

Above: Avalanches on the Milford Road, Fiordland National Park
Left: Winter snow, central Southern Alps, Westland National Park

branches of high country trees and gives lakes the heavy, forbidding stillness of great mirrors. Winter is the starred ice on toffee-coloured puddles and the crisp crackle of frost underfoot. Winter is the gold reflected in the wide black flow of the Waikato River at dawn. Winter is the nap of tussock grasses surrounded by snow remnants blowing silver before the wind.

As the land cools down, so do coastal waters. Winter's storms stir up the sea, mixing warm surface waters with cold southern currents to create a uniform coolness. Less sunlight means less photosynthesis. This in turn means less plankton and algae are produced, so the sea itself is a lot clearer. Many fish now move out of harbours and bays in search of warmer currents. Marlin, tuna, sunfish and smaller sharks travel towards tropical waters. Moki, however, choose to move in the opposite direction and into colder water.

Fishing boats go after deep-sea fish, harvesting hake, ling, southern blue whiting and orange roughy. Crayfishers are out lowering their crayfish traps onto ocean beds. The sea is silver-grey and glassy on calm days under the low sun. Waves break in smooth curls with little foam. Rain is never far away in winter,

however. There are also days when the air feels wet even though it isn't raining. Moisture lurks, placing drops of water on the ends of gorse spines in coastal areas and encouraging wraiths of mist to spin up out of forests. The ground is waterlogged, old weatherboards retain the damp and airports may be fog-bound for part of the day.

Another cold front begins to flow up the country from the deep south. The wind increases, keening and sighing. Pebbles click over boulders. Then the salt-laden sea winds whip along beaches pluming the

Above: Winter dawn, north of Kaikoura
Left: Willow tree, South Canterbury

writing manes, sea-wet locks tossing and flexing.

When winds are strong the surf is roused to grandeur, all eddy and chop, foam and fury. Boats head for shelter. Sea swells of up to six metres in Cook Strait force ferry crossings to be cancelled. On the exposed west coast of the South Island the sea whips up like white meringue: thick suds plaster the beaches. The froth is a species of sea algae, agitated by the dynamic interaction of wind and waves.

Sheets of rain sluice the windows of south-facing buildings. Wind gusts tear holes in the rain. As the fury of a storm increases, pinwheels of water begin spraying from the rocky outcrops of hillsides. Torrents, waterfalls and rivers fling themselves from high places, fearless and irresistible. Water courses downhill to flood roads and block drains. Soggy soil syndrome begins to manifest itself in the form of erosion, a widespread hazard of New Zealand hill farming country. As H. Guthrie-Smith wrote in *Tutira*, his 1921 farming classic, 'hillsides spew forth mud ... sometimes a whole hillside will wrinkle and slide like snow melting off a roof.'

These earth slips and scourings flush rocks, pebbles and silt out of gaunt hill ranges and down to the coast where they will be ground down to gravel

sand, bending the trees and scorching the grasses. The march of rollers sweeping in from the sea starts to surge. Waves begin to thrash, driving up against rocks. Driblets of tumbling foam are swept back in streaming veils. Bull-kelp boils in the surf attached by holdfasts to rocks, whipping its fronds into a lather of long

Above: Winter morning, Fiordland National Park
Right: Falling snow, Lewis Pass

or sand. The strength of the sea then shovels it back up again between the headlands.

The accelerated sweeping away of great chunks of volcanic soil, a direct result of forest clearing and over-grazing, carves deep gouges creating scars in the landscape, especially in the North Island. The vast aprons of shingle decorating the eastern slopes of mountains in Marlborough, Canterbury and Otago are also prone to move in heavy rain, causing further massive slips. This working loose of fragments of greywacke sandstone, a gradual process of natural erosion and a testament to the power of wind and water, is counterbalanced by the slow uplift of land caused by the movement of the earth's tectonic plates.

On exposed coasts, sea spray mingles with driving rain to create one blinding wall of water. Windows of houses, baches and cribs become coated with a sticky rime which can rapidly rust exposed metal. River gravels that are being carried seawards roar and roll, to and fro with the waves. Native timber logs float down rivers during storms and end up on beaches where they may be salvaged by woodcarvers and furniture-makers. Cairns of tangled driftwood form around river mouths, having been flung back up on shore by

Tangaroa the sea-god, bearing witness to their rainforest of origin.

After the brawling southerly blows itself out, you wake in the morning to blue sky and brilliant sunshine. The air is clear, the roiling silver of the incoming tide ripples with light, the surface of both land and sea sparkles with a renewed sense of optimism.

The rain-laden gales often cause a mass inland migration of sea birds. Birds who are slow to move may be seen tacking against the force of the wind. Sheltered microclimates also attract birds. In the Kukumoa area, in the Bay of Plenty north-east of Opotiki, cattle egrets winter over between April and

Above: Sheep grazing, Springs Junction
Left: Beech forest, Te Urewera National Park

October protected from the southerlies by hill ranges. While many forest birds move down from the ranges into lowland forests, some waterfowl remain on upland lakes to conduct winter courtships. The paradise duck, its black head glossed with green, may be seen paddling through the still water of a lake looking for a mate. While most lizards, including the tuatara, are hibernating, the skink lizards of Central Otago emerge on sunny days to bask and frolic on rocks protruding from the snow.

Farmers usually welcome rain because the grasslands need it for steady growth, which in turn means fatter sheep. However, as endless rain alternates with pelting hail or frosts and light dustings of snow, paddocks become muddy troughs and farmers turn to feeding out slabs of hay from summer stores. Many dairy farmers spell their pastures at this time and dry off their herds.

Too much rain and floodwaters may pour over spillways, causing stock to battle their way to higher ground. Stock are often on the move in winter, seeking shelter. Farmers move round after them in gumboots. On high country stations they may have to go out and snowrake (rescue sheep by making tracks in the

snow) wethers in the aftermath of a blizzard. Sheep, belly-deep in snow, sodden, the colour of dirty hail, can start suffering from exposure. In Southland, Otago and Canterbury, farmers may put stock in semi-protected areas: against stone walls, under trees or even house them in barns. In most parts of the country horses wear blankets or tarpaulins when they are out

Above: Te Paki sand dunes, Ninety Mile Beach, Northland
Left: Kingfisher – these birds move to lower levels during winter, nearer food supplies

Above: Southern Alps
Left: Lake Hawea, Central Otago

of their stables.

In the South Island, snow on mountain peaks refrigerates the winter air so that farms receive crisp frosts. In the North Island, frosts are a frequent occurrence after days and nights of next to no wind accompanied by fine clear weather. In mid-winter the hard freeze arrives. Morning fog may freeze and turn into rime ice, a fine crystalline substance clinging to the air. Wafers of clear ice form on river shallows. Water droplets turn into ice capsules which bead number eight wire. Ponds ice over. The suffused violet twilight of a winter evening often betokens a hard frost to follow. The thin white fur of the frost runs across the landscape, making grass brittle and white. It encrusts shrubs and plants with ice crystals on clear, dry mornings as faint wreaths of smoke arise from kitchen fires. On such mornings the dogs in their kennels rattle their chains in greeting but do not venture forth.

Most primary producers limit themselves to the performance of essential tasks. Kiwifruit is harvested in the Bay of Plenty and Hawke's Bay in early winter. Gardeners plant out trees and roses (the cold promotes vigorous root growth), sow broad beans and plant garlic. Viticulturalists prune their vines. Orchardists welcome late winter frosts because the

frosts promote the flowering and fruiting of apricot, peach and nectarine trees. Sometimes, on a clear winter's day, curls of black smoke may be seen rising from a run-holder's burn-off of bracken.

In the aftermath of a snowstorm the epic panorama of the Southern Alps is a dark monochrome. The landscape is minimalist. Snow falls steadily creating a world which is mostly composed of silence and whiteness. Cold winds blow the air clean and the high alpine country becomes an empire of ice. Waterfalls and streams slow to a trickle or ice up completely. Frozen water hangs in stalactites or forms an almost invisible skin over rocks. Glaciers reassert themselves

Above: Winter climbing in Spencer Mountains, Nelson Lakes National Park
Left: Tasman Glacier, Aoraki/Mount Cook National Park

as solid rivers. Occasionally there is the sound of blocks of ice falling. Strands of snow and ice stand out against black rocks.

Colours change on the mountains as day progresses towards evening. The Remarkables under snow are a poem in white, bathed pink and orange at sunset, then, turning a deep purple as the turquoise sky takes on a darker blue and a thick glitter of stars pastes itself across the clear night sky.

The white blitz of winter in Canterbury's Mackenzie Country delivers savage snowstorms. It is a region of extremes, like the volcanic plateau of the central North island and the Central Otago high country. These places have the highest summer temperatures and the lowest winter temperatures in New Zealand. Sometimes they have the highest and lowest temperatures in the country on the same winter's day. But when the weather lifts, the clarity seems surreal as leaping peaks of mountains reflect in still lakes and rivers spill towards the sea across the Canterbury Plains in lacy silver scribbles. The skeletal branches of trees seem to be spelling out nature's secrets in a language we can't quite read.

The winter solstice occurs between the 20th and the

Above: Beech tree, Mount Cook Village
Left: Avenue of trees, Arrowtown, Central Otago

23rd of June. In some parts of the country it is acknowledged with all-night outdoor music festivals around a bonfire. In Dunedin there is a polar plunge. This mid-winter swim with prizes for best costumes takes place on St Kilda Beach at noon on the Sunday closest to the shortest day.

Ski-fields open in late June/early July, depending on when the first good snow-dump of the season arrives. Skiers flock to slopes on the great volcanic mountains in the centre of the North Island, or to the main divide of the South Island. There, the chains of mountains escalate to meet clouds, peaks plunging 'their icy heads into space' as poet Charles Brasch wrote.

On the ski-fields you can be burnt by the glare of the sun; unless you shield your eyes you risk snow-blindness. Cross-country skiers are advised to be cautious. More people die from avalanches in New Zealand per head of population than in any other country. The weather can turn very quickly as the storm cycle repeats itself.

The sudden arrival of white-out conditions makes access roads impassable. Many roads, especially in the southern half of the South Island or in the centre of the North Island, may be temporarily closed, except to motorists with chains. Graders and snowploughs emerge; road workers are kept busy spreading grit on mushy snow. Hardy thrillseekers kayak down river torrents, or take to mid-winter surfing. As the cold wind whips colour into cheeks, children build snow-men, make snow-caves, start snowball fights or skid along slushy pavements on home-made carts or on rubber inner tubes.

Every few years there is a big snow and Southland, Otago and Canterbury are blanketed from sea to summit. Hospital and school boilers are kept going full blast; delivery and service people venture out cautiously; some stay snugly indoors feeding logs which were chainsawed up over summer and autumn into blazing, log fires. There may be skaters out on iced-over dams, or groups playing the ancient Scottish sport of curling. Of course, winter is also the heart of the rugby season, and parks and domains are packed at weekends with teams of players of all ages, supported by parents, relatives and friends. At such times it seems that rugby goal-posts have suddenly sprouted up on every second paddock in small towns everywhere.

The smoggy, lumpen sprawl of Christchurch is one of our urban symbols of winter. The city seems to

Right: Snowboarder

turn vaporous as days dawn monotonously grey. The city's location in low drained swampland hemmed in behind the Port Hills leads to temperature inversions where the bottom layer of air, being colder and damper than the air above it, stagnates. Before the introduction of fire regulations, Christchurch had a serious air pollution problem that was a direct result of domestic and industrial coal fires. Even today, air pollution and frosty nights conspire to trap smog.

In the depths of winter, New Zealand cities generally snivel with influenza, despite a regime of inoculations. Houses are warmed with electric heaters, central heating, double insulation and double glazing. People are warmed with the aid of hot water bottles, electric blankets, linen sheets and winceyette pyjamas. Workers on the land clothe themselves in wool: thick woollen socks, woollen balaclavas, wool shirts, Swanndris. Office workers wear woollen vests beneath wool suits.

Climatic variations, though, mean some regions have a relatively mild winter. In Nelson the spurs of the Motueka Valley make the north-facing province something of a suntrap in winter. On the same latitude as the Hawke's Bay fruitbowl, its high ranges protect it from the Tasman seaboard's fierce westerlies.

The exposed isthmus of Auckland rarely has frosts, but sometimes there is a steady succession of squalls when it seems to rain for weeks on end. Flags, banners and canopies flap in the stiff easterly or westerly breezes which bring showers, rainstorms and dull days succeeded by the occasional brilliant burst of fine weather. Areas with clay subsoil become claggy and boggy. However, those areas with volcanic soils that drain easily are green and lush.

The Waikato countryside also stays green, though land trampled by cattle turns muddy and lingering fog

Above: Cemetery, Fairlie, South Canterbury
Left: Snow blanket over foothills and mountains, near Fairlie, South Canterbury

country: a land of bare, scraped rock, volcanic cinders and hard black lava, and loose scoria and pumice powdered to sand by centuries of weathering. Bonsai forests of totara trees grow at high altitudes on these bleak reaches, beneath the snow cones of the Tongariro National Park. At lower altitudes in this volcanic region there are vents in the earth from which geysers blow like the safety valves of steam engines. This is a realm of grumbling mud-pools and hissing steam, of simmering cauldrons dimpled by ice-cold rain. Wisps of ice-cloud swirl over thermal springs. The whole landscape is stained with trace elements of earth's fire and sky's ice.

To the north is Rotorua, where the air smells perpetually of sulphur, and gaping fissures plunge deep into the body of the earth. You may bathe in the sulphuretted waters of the thermal pools – some are alkaline, some acidic – and benefit from the healing properties of the solutions of mineral deposits which contain mercury, iodine, silica and sulphur. Around you, mud-pools bubble and snap like boiling porridge, while geysers roar, throwing scalding water high into the sky. White hail may suddenly pelt down out of the sky. You soak in the heat, the steam from your body rising into the icy air.

and damp is common in low-lying areas adjacent to the Waikato River. Towards the Waikato River's headwaters on the volcanic plateau the air becomes dry. There is a crystalline quality to the light in this upland area that makes far-off things look close.

Across the volcanic plateau ice forms in shady areas on frosty mornings, and there are sometimes snowfalls. State Highway One between Waiouru and Taihape is usually closed a couple of times each winter. Cold winds howl across, and fog, mist and cloud descend frequently. In the west, Mt Taranaki clasps a dark mist around herself like a cloak.

The heartland of the North Island is pumice

Above: Shed at Ohakune, Central North Island
Right: Shelterbelt shrouded in winter mist, Waikato

Top: Morning catch of hapuku, East Cape
Above: Winter gale on Otago Harbour
Right: Super 12 Rugby

The traditional Maori new year began in the depths of winter. Matariri (the Pleiades) reappears in the Milky Way late in June, at the winter solstice. Its arrival symbolised the turning of Takurua (the star Sirius) towards the warmer weather. Takurua was the star-god who brought cold, frost and snow. His name meant "Winter".

In Maori cosmology, Ra, the sun-god, had two wives. He pays attention for half the year to Hine-takurua the Winter-Woman in the south, and dances attendance on Hine-raumati, the Summer-Woman in the north for the other half of the year. Ra begins his journey towards Hine-raumati at the winter solstice. It is she who dwelt on the land and who was associated with the foodbasket of the kumara harvest in the Maori calendar. Hine-takurua's domain was kaimoana – the foodbasket of the sea. In winter when the ground was too cold for cultivation, people lived on the autumn harvest of kumara, and also hunted birds – tui, kaka, kereru – and caught eels. Though nights drew in early and days were short this was also the season of Tumatauenga, the god of war. Young warriors went on raiding parties or took revenge (utu) against other tribes.

The sun sets and the constellations rise. Sagitta-

rius, Scorpius, Libra, Virgo, Leo, Pisces, Aquarius and Capricornus begin their long arc of travel across the night sky, star upon star receding into the deep night of winter. The lights of the aurora australis are seen lingering after dusk. In the North Island they glow red and in the South Island they tinge the sky green with a reddish-purple afterglow. Stretching up, the rays sometimes spread into a pattern, radiating out like wide spokes of a wheel. As August moves towards its end the weather remains cold and sharp, but the promise of spring is in the air. In the New Zealand forest the clematis, manuka and kowhai are preparing to flower.

Above: Mist rising off rapids, Huka Falls, Taupo
Left: Wellington harbour and central city

SPRING

TAKURUA

In spring the land dances on tiptoe to the rattle of flax pods, the rustle of flax leaves, the chant of bird song, the jigging strains of river music, and the upper registers of the singing wind as it flings hanks of cloud through the sky. September 1 marks the first official day of spring, but the season itself is sometimes late, sometimes early. There's the occasional false start some years, with warm mid-winter weather spurring flowers into sudden bloom. Other signs appear gradually: the first calls of the shining cuckoo (pipiwharauroa) returned from the tropics signal the promise of warmth, while, for a few more weeks, southerly winds continue to bring dustings of snow. Then the grey warbler (riroriro) takes up the theme, its musical trill ushering in the new season.

Just as a tossed handful of earth might stir a geothermal hot pool into effervescence, the turn of the seasons stirs the land into rebirth. Cloud begins to clear from both the mountains to the south and from the white cones of the central North Island volcanoes. The pure drizzle that has hung like a grey scrim veiling headlands and coastal hills for weeks suddenly

Left: The koru form of an emerging fern

vanishes. The wet, dank bush of the forests shakes off the incessant plash of rain and begins to renew itself as everything soggy either falls apart or begins to dry out. A rainbow stands out briefly against dark clouds. On these first fickle spring days the precious gold of sunshine is frequently interrupted by the flashing silver of rain.

In high southern places the wind can still cut razor-like through your clothing as it blows across the tussock. Icicles in the mountains continue to shine like rows of long white fingernails, but the inevitable thaw is beginning. In the rainforests of the north the bush exudes the essences of decomposition: a top note of freshness, a middle note of first flowers, and a bass note of leaf mould. Early blossom clothes the trees with promise. Now, in the words of the Maori proverb: ka whakaniho nga mea katoa o te whenua i konei – all things of the earth begin to sprout.

In late August, bush clematis begins flowering, looking like white stars scattered across the dark greenery. Known by Maori as Puawananga, this plant was regarded as a gift from the sky gods, and as the daughter of two important stars in the ancient Maori calendar – Rehua (the red Antares in the constellation of Scorpio) and Puanga (Rigel, the bright white star at the top of the constellation of Orion). She was the spirit of spring, sent by other atua (protective spirits) to signal the approach of summer. The white shawl-like appearance of the flowers led early colonists to call the clematis "The Lady of October", her mildly fragrant flowers often being at their most profuse in October, before falling away in November.

The starry masses of clematis are soon joined by other native blooms – the creamy-pink flowers of the kamahi, hinau's rusty-tinged blossoms, kumarahou's petals of dusty gold, and, most strikingly, the kowhai's golden locks. For ancient Maori the flowering of the kowhai was another harbinger: they used it to set the time for kumara planting. Now the tui puts in an appearance, darting between branches seeking

Above: Tui, native New Zealand nectar-feeding bird
Right: Kanuka and totara forest, freshened by spring rain

kowhai nectar. The tui, looking smart with its metallic green plumage, purplish sheen and two small white puffs of neck feathers, can sip nectar from a kowhai flower as delicately as any Ponsonby Road café-goer enjoying a small cup of espresso.

By late September, flowers begin to cling to the branches of manuka and kanuka shrubs and whole hillsides appear frosted, the whiteness of the flowers offset by dark leaves and brownish stems encrusted with sooty mould. The acrid resinous odour of crushed manuka leaf is redolent of the bush and has led to manuka being known as the tea-tree – pioneers used to brew up the leaves.

The soused rainforest – the colour of pounamu – seems to exude a liquid emerald essence. Every leaf, twig and tree bole is drenched and dripping, a green womb of fecundity. A superabundance of efflorescence seems to emanate from the forest floor of mosses, algae, lichens and filmy ferns glowing green and occasionally orange. As climbers flower overhead, leafy branches weave a loose latticework to produce a twilight gloom at ground level. There on the ground strings of filmy ferns hang from logs. A commonwealth of ferns – piu piu, ponga, mamaku, rauaruhe – begin uncurling and sprouting, while green-hooded orchids

bloom, and mushrooms and other fungi flourish. The air is heavy with the sweet scent of the horopito. In the cloud forests of the alpine regions, the trees are festooned with shaggy tresses and trailing beards of thick mosses. The tramper or hunter has to negotiate thickets of vines, networks of roots, and a riot of exuberant growth.

Yet this is also a landscape of ecological dispossession, affording scant sanctuary to indigenous birds and other creatures: small predators – stoats, ferrets, weasels, rats – stalk the undergrowth, while overhead a vast army of possums is munching its way through the bush canopy.

Above: Kowhai blossoms
Left: Flowering kowhai, Mission Bay, Lake Taupo

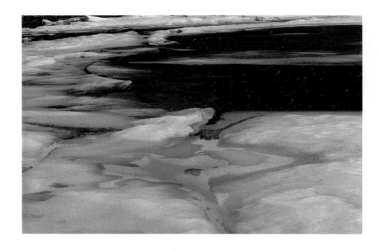

Emerging from the primeval shadow of the bush can feel like arriving in another country. On the cleared lowlands the gorse is blooming, carrying a coconut-like smell on the wind. Willows are sprouting green alongside rivers. For many, the white flowers of hawthorn hedges are symbolic of a European-style spring, even as the golden flames of kowhai are extinguished one by one.

Yet the whole landscape at this time of the year is really a gloriously diverse floral display, from the suburban gardens and city parks with their hosts of yellow daffodils and scarlet tulips, to the blossoming orchards which bedeck sheltered plains and valleys,

the gold and rose of broom and sweet briar in the high country, the daisies and lupin of roadside verges, and the mountain buttercups of alpine meadows. All this colour seems reflected in the sunsets of the eastern sky. There reefs of gold frame bursts of cloud turning pink or flaming crimson before fading to black. The colours of the sky prefigure the pink flush of apples, the gold gleam of apricots and the dark red of cherries.

However, such bucolic harmony is not the whole story. New Zealand is a wind-swept country. Spring and autumn are generally times when winds are strongest, especially during the equinoctial gales. (Spring equinox is between 20 and 23 September). New Zealand, rising straight up out of the sea in the latitudes known as the Roaring Forties, collides with westerly ocean winds that have swept across the Tasman encountering no resistance for more than 1000 kilometres. This sparring with the elements helps to shape a wild and vigorous climate that always seems to be in a state of change.

The winds of the Roaring Forties, trapped by the ramparts of mountain ranges, are funnelled across Cook Strait, shaking and trembling the shelterbelts of

Above: Spring snow melt, Arrowsmith Range, Canterbury
Right: Paradise ducklings arrive as the snow departs

pines and macrocarpas along the way. Winds scoot up and down scalloped hills – all bony ridges and narrow valleys. They soar over the vertical limit of the Southern Alps and, having dumped what sometimes seems like an ocean of water on the West Coast, heat up and drive down onto the eastern slopes in the shape of the formidable nor'wester. The nor'wester is a dry wind ready to brawl with the moist southerlies driving up from the southern ocean through Otago, Canterbury, Marlborough, Wellington and the Manawatu. In the lower North Island, westerlies, funnelling through the Manawatu Gorge and between the Tararua and Ryan Ranges, can buffet the whole countryside with crosswinds. Wellington and Invercargill are New Zealand's windiest cities.

But while the westerlies, the nor'westerlies and the southerlies are quarrelling, the land is warming and the snows are melting. Soon, swollen with meltwater, the rivers are in full spate. They tumble down from steep mountains, turning into helterskelter water-chutes. When sudden rain-squalls strike the mountains they create white threads of waterfalls which seam rock faces of terrain that is deeply faulted, buckled and stretched. Water bounces as it falls into plunge pools and onward down gullies in ever-joining

Top: Tulips, Hagley Park, Christchurch
Above: Camelia
Left: Catkins on willows

creeks that eventually form surging water serpents which hurry towards the sea with a roar. In Fiordland (one of the wettest places on earth) the tea-coloured rivers form a murky freshwater lens on the surface of the sea in the inner Sounds.

Across the Canterbury Plains, the silvery-blue lizard twists of rivers spread dynamically over shingle fans. In the North Island, the deep, dark-green waters of the Waikato River, are smooth-surfaced, but beneath the surface, eddies and whirlpools can be glimpsed spinning silently and churning into themselves. On the East Cape, after heavy spring rains, silt loads are carried down the Waipaoa River leaving slips and slumps on the steep hills of the Gisborne District. On some flood plains, flash floods can scour out new channels then leave tides of silt caking in the sun after they recede. Within Maoritanga rivers are living beings coexisting, physically and spiritually, if not peacefully, with the iwi who inhabit their environs. Thus the flowing glaze of a river conceals legends.

When a river reaches the sea it may encounter a king-tide – the combination of a high spring tide and an onshore wind. Spring tides may leave behind feathers, crab shells, fish, twigs, branches, even whole trees, beached against the land, while big swells continue to whip up a salt haze with slow but persistent corrosive force.

In Northland the seascape is part of the landscape. The Tasman Sea's huge surf crashes onto one long beach which is gradually moving inshore, creating sand dunes driven on by westerlies. The eastern side of the Northland peninsula is made up of an intricate pattern of sheltered coves, bays, estuaries and islands. Here, spring is not a season of dynamic change, but one of subtle transition from cool to warm.

On the sub-tropical West Coast of the South Island, it is also sometimes difficult to tell when spring has arrived. This is a place where people spend a lot of time listening to different kinds of rain: fine floating rain, gentle tiny rain, steady pattering rain, strong drumming rain, rain falling in heavy sheets. Then a fine day arrives so clear, silent and still, saying spring is here at last.

Towards the end of September the mournful cry of many birds can be heard – the sooty shearwaters (titi or muttonbirds) are arriving from the northern hemisphere. They number in their millions and nest in huge colonies on the islands of Foveaux Strait. The

Left: The beginnings of a spring gale, Cook Strait

sooty shearwaters lay a single egg which hatches into a grey-downed chick. Fed with regurgitated fish oil by both parents, the chick puts on weight fast and soon becomes a little tub of fat. They are a traditional food source for southern Maori who grab them in their burrows in the autumn before they are fully fledged.

New Zealand is the seabird capital of the world, home to a vast array of different species. On Otago Peninsula a royal albatross pops up on the buoyant wind as if shot out of a cannon, before wheeling and gliding away on enormous extended wings. Taiaroa Head is the only mainland nesting place for the albatross, which begins nest-building in October, lays a single egg in November, and hatches a chick in late January. Penguins, black-backed gulls, prions and many other birds share the southern coast. The tiny white-faced storm petrel doesn't nest here but spends a season feeding. This delicate sea bird seems to dance above the sea as it feeds, establishing a harmony between the updraught of the waves and the beating of its wings.

Gannets and shags, however, plummet straight down into deep water, as do shags, disappearing momentarily before bobbing back up to the surface with fish flapping in their beaks. Amongst the bustle

of coastal birds, shags can be noticed as they spread their distinctive heavy wings out to dry.

The Christchurch wetlands are home to paradise shelducks, scaup (papango) and some 1400 pukeko, all busy breeding in the spring. Perhaps when the paddling ducks zestfully fling showers of spray over their shoulders they are acknowledging spring. Further north, diving petrels have returned to the islands of the Hauraki Gulf to breed. In the distance they may

Above: Spring lamb
Left: Lush spring growth on farmland, Waitahuna, Southland

*Above: Hooker sea lions,
ashore for breeding,
Auckland Islands
Left: Gibson albatross
chick, Adams Island,
Auckland Islands
Right: Royal albatross,
Campbell Island*

observe Auckland sailing yachts skimming over the surface of the sea like mollymawks.

On bird-crowded estuaries, troops of bar-tailed godwits, newly arrived from Siberia, are marching along the mudflats to feed on pipi banks, small insects and crustaceans. The godwits, along with about a dozen other species of waders migrate to New Zealand in the southern spring, feeding in the shallow harbours before flying off northwards again in the autumn.

Other birds too are on the wing. The creak and whirr of the lumbering keruru may be heard in gardens and green belts as this large native wood pigeon descends to feed on the leaves of both exotic and native trees and gathers material to build its simple nest. The bellbird (korimako) is breeding, as is the endangered kaka, once one of the country's most prolific birds. The graceful white heron (kotuku), a national symbol, is nesting in a kahikatea forest in south Westland, its only breeding site in New Zealand. While magpies nest and chatter in the macrocarpas, sparrows in the suburbs squabble and fend off the aggression of mynas and the nosiness of swallows.

Whitebait. You have to be quick to spot them slipping

Far left:
Kahikatea,
Arahaki Lagoon,
Central North
Island
Left: Native forest
of dense tree
ferns, North
Westland

through. They are the spawn of inanga or native trout returning from the sea, flitting upriver in shreds and patches and sometimes dense shoals. You'll find whitebaiters motoring to rivers such as the Waimakariri and the Mokau in spring to set nets on the incoming tide. Catches are variable, but the dedicated whitebaiters go out regardless, sometimes in old bombs, sometimes in late-model four-wheel drives. It's a rugged make-do culture, incorporating nets, handy buckets and any old bit of tarpaulin or wooden pallet to help create some sort of shelter while waiting for the whitebait to run the gauntlet, guided by primordial instinct and seeking safety in numbers.

Round the coasts, too, the grey ghost-like forms of dolphins begin to be seen as the season advances flitting through the ripples of the sun-splashed green brine, their dark skins gleaming as they leap and plunge. Deeper beneath them in the gloom, whales

Above: Fresh whitebait from the Paringa River, South Westland
Left: Whitebait set nets on river's edge, South Westland

are on the move, migrating to other feeding pastures.

The small, somewhat shy native bees are emerging from their solitary sandburrows, and assorted newly-hatched butterflies are fluttering their wings. In late spring bees are sometimes used to help out with pollination in orchards. In the Bay of Plenty, thousands of beehives are moved (at night to make sure all bees are present) into the kiwifruit growing district.

In Central Otago orchardists place hundreds of smudge pots outside to burn oil and keep late frosts at bay. Spring is also an anxious time for other primary producers. The sudden return of a cold snap could threaten the lives of recently shorn sheep or newborn lambs who are barely able to wobble after their mother ewes.

Nelson's apple and hop growers and Hawke's Bay fruit growers scan the skies for signs of thunderstorms or hailstorms. On dairy farms around the country, except possibly very wet regions like Southland, farmers are counting on spring rains to bring on the lush pastures needed for fattening up lambs and allowing calving cows to make milk.

Spring is also a bugle call to the outdoor enthusiast. The trout fishing season gets underway in those places where it isn't already underway, and rock-climbers, boaties and canoeists head outside in droves. While some are content to travel up Canterbury's now deep rivers by jet-boat, others are in training to get from one coast of the South Island to the other by running over mountains, kayaking down the Waimakariri, and cycling across the plains, as if driven by the prevailing wind.

In October, draughts of spicy rhododendron fragrance fill home gardens in cooler areas of the country. While the rhododendron festivals of Taranaki and Dunedin recognise the colourful clamour of the rhododendron flower, the more general blossoming of spring is acknowledged in the nation's fruitbowl capitals of Alexandra and Hastings with their respective blossom festivals. While hay-fever sufferers may be found reaching for their antihistamines as spring breezes thrash pollen about, others are enjoying the presence of massed banks of wisteria, azaleas and the many other flowers in bloom.

In Christchurch the week after the Melbourne Cup (the trans-Tasman event that brings both nations to a sweepstake standstill on the afternoon of the first Tuesday in November) is the week of both the DB Draught New Zealand Trotting Cup at Addington

Left: Morning milking, Golden Bay

Above: Marae framed by spring rhododendrons in bloom
Left : Lawn bowls, Gisborne

Raceway, and the Canterbury Agricultural and Pastoral Show, where traditional events like woodchopping, shearing competitions and livestock parades have these days been joined by fashion parades of fine wool garments and displays of boutique farm enthusiasms.

In spring the washed air glitters. Spring is the crackle of ice breaking up into meltwater. Spring is beach sand scuffed by the webbed feet of sea birds. Spring seems to pick open the light locked inside greenstone or kauri gum. Spring is a rainbow over a teardrop lake ruffled by a storm. Spring is when water, earth and sky realign themselves, and when the fire mountains of the volcanic plateau balance the forbidding bulk of the ice mountains in the south. Both shed snow but also keep their distance, stern as gods in a pantheon. Spring is the sea streaked lavender, the land breaking rom the horizon a deeper purple and strands of cloud a feathery golden-white, the colour of toetoe plumes. The warming breeze as spring ends is a benediction as soft as breath.

Top: Spring harvest, Gisborne
Above: Rows of lettuces ready for markets, Gisborne
Right: Sheep on Kaikoura Peninsula